MOMENTA ART

EXHIBITIONS 1995 THROUGH 1999

CONTENTS

me

INTRODUCTION

Momenta Art is a not-for-profit exhibition space dedicated to promoting the work of emerging artists. Through two person shows artists are provided with separate project rooms and the distinct opportunity to present a substantial body of work. For most of these artists, this is their first opportunity to exhibit in New York outside a group show. For each exhibition we publish a newsletter which provides further information about the work exhibited in our project rooms and also lists other local galleries. The newsletter also contains a map of art spaces in the area, so for those unfamiliar with Williamsburg, Momenta is an excellent first stop in Brooklyn.

Momenta Art has been in existence since 1986, beginning with group shows in donated, temporary spaces in Philadelphia, and managed by artists James Mills, Eric Heist, Donna Czapiga, Christina LaSala, and Timothy Aubry. While in Philadelphia, Momenta provided early exposure to such notable artists as Karen Kilimnik, Katy Schimert, Paula Hayes, Jim Hodges, and Virgil Marti. Momenta relocated to New York in 1992, presenting group exhibitions in temporary, rented spaces in Soho, and publishing multiple artworks. At these venues we exhibited, among others, Lucky DeBellevue, Tony Feher, Marlene McCarty, Barbara Pollock, and Sue Williams. We then opened our current, permanent space in Williamsburg, Brooklyn in March 1995, co-directed by Eric Heist and Laura Parnes, continuing our mission to bring exposure to and increasing the public's awareness of emerging and underrepresented artsists. Although Momenta has gone through several transformations, we have managed to remain an artist-run, not-for-profit space. This is an unusual and difficult task in New York City, where expenses are high and fund-raising is crucial to the survival of a space. By keeping our program small and focused, Momenta Art remains a space run by and for artists.

This catalog includes all the exhibitions that we have presented between the opening of our Williamsburg, Brooklyn, space in March 1995 and May 1999. The importance of artist-run exhibition spaces in Williamsburg has reached historic proportions. Because we are located in a neighborhood that contains one of the largest populations of artists in the United States, we are in a unique position to be a catalyst for discussion throughout the artistic community. We decided to publish this as a reference for this period while contextualizing our project within the ongoing history of not-for-profit art spaces.

The writing in the catalog is collaborative unless otherwise noted. Generally the artists submitted statements at the time of their exhibitions. These statements were edited by Laura Parnes and submitted to Eric Heist for a final edit. We would like to thank Michael Ashkin and Lisa Alberts for proofreading and Bill Arning for his wonderful essay. We are grateful to Anne Young for providing advice and support for the project, as well as Jenny Frances Martin. Special thanks to Sarah Vogwill for her excellent design work and patience.

Generous support for this catalog has come from the Florence J. Gould Foundation, Ms. Agnes Gund and Mr. Daniel Shapiro, and The Heathcote Foundation, to whom we extend our thanks. We are grateful to the artists for their help in gathering materials and documentation. We would also like to thank all the members of the Board of Directors for their help and advice concerning the project.

Eric Heist/Laura Parnes
Co-Directors

A.K.A. MOMENT(A)

We cannot just assume the necessity of the continuing existence of what we in North America call alternative spaces, a.k.a. artist-run spaces (artists space for short), a.k.a. not-for-profits a.k.a. parallel galleries (the Canadian term), a.k.a. whatever the next term will be. We must always be checking their pulses – examining how they function within the larger art system, locally and globally and thereby see if they are fulfilling the complex tasks that we expect of them. It's a fair guess that the number of different names we have for these spaces is indicative of the multitude of roles we expect them to fulfill.

In considering the case of Momenta, we have a unique version. Momenta, the lovechild of the artists Eric Heist and Laura Parnes is the only such space in Williamsburg, Brooklyn. This little corner of the borough has been for several years the largest tribal gathering of artists in the history of the world. This is definitely true in terms of the sheer numbers of participants. Also notable is the wild diversity of coexisting styles and diverse disciplines and the intoxicating babble of such a mass of cutting-edge propositions about what art can or should be being offered for our provocation every day in those few dozen blocks.

In my years of working in the field I have articulated in many ways the special things that spaces like Momenta bring to the plethora of other available art-sites. After a few years on the other side of the equation, working as a critic – in a sense a meta-viewer, an over-informed surrogate audience member – I see Momenta as a lens, as a way of looking at art. Every art-viewing situation has other built-in, extra-artistic factors that influence how we experience the objects before us. While it is simplistic to say that commercial galleries' imperative to sell is a negative influence on our experience, since, after all, uncollected work is rarely preserved, one is aware that some shows happen because the work is "What people are buying" (not by definition the same as conservative). Galleries must also try to present work in such a way as to knock the viewer senseless. Every work must be presented as a masterwork, and while dealers are usually very nice to us critics, their jobs are clearly not to facilitate critical debate.

When museums, which admittedly do not regularly work with living artists, do venture into the field, such as MOMA's project room series, they cannot help but bring the weighty stamp of approval, the guarantee of cultural authority to artworks when those works hang in the hall built by Picasso. This remains true even when the curators mean them to be debatable propositions and not carved-in-stone statements.

Momenta's stated mission is "to promote the work of emerging and underrepresented artists." The underlying theme is one of fairness, "If they are underrepresented now lets see what we can do to make them fairly represented." It is that sense of disinterestedness that one knows and remembers in looking at Momenta's shows. Also in using the word "emerging" is the fact that there is not and should not be any claim for "greatness" for the selected artists. The space, in choosing who it will include in its programming, makes no claim beyond "We've been thinking this is interesting, do you agree?" a fundamentally generous position inviting the audience's full participation. This does not mean I have not seen work that I thought was great there; I have, but Momenta leaves it up to us for judgment.

That does not mean that Momenta needs to have no criteria and thus avoid judgments of quality. Indeed, their audience, made up 90 percent of art practitioners, is the toughest audience in the world. Two lousy shows in a row and they do not come back a third time. But there is a difference between showing dreck, which Momenta has not done, and allowing an emerging artist to try something new and nobly fail, which they have indeed done, and should continue to risk doing. Trust me, the Williamsburgers know the difference. They must of course also please the space's funders, who also know the difference.

Momenta has passed its adolescence and is now in the strange world of being an established alternative space, joining its five older Manhattan bound sister-spaces: Exit Art, White Columns, Art in General, Thread Waxing Space and Artists Space. What does it mean for the future? Williamsburg has oodles of artist-run spaces today, and some may actually go the route of Momenta, getting not for-profit status and making it permanent, but even for a dedicated art scavenger like me, I can never find them all. To understand the significance of that, we must switch to the other side of the equation: the artists who have shown, will show, or hope to show at Momenta.

Because Williamsburg is today a well-known art scene, curators, collectors, and critics from around the world make it out there. Momenta can play a part in the hopes and dreams of artists so well only because everyone goes there because it is stable, so everyone knows where it is and that it ain't going nowhere. So make it your first stop and they will even give you a handout of all the other temporary spaces that Momenta helps nurture.

In a nutshell, as an alternative, not-for-profit, artist-run, parallel space where everyone wants to show, Momenta is the unique impartial, deliberate, non-authoritative lens for considering the crazy density of art propositions in rapid motion, one cultural Moment(a) at a time.

Bill Arning
NYC 1999

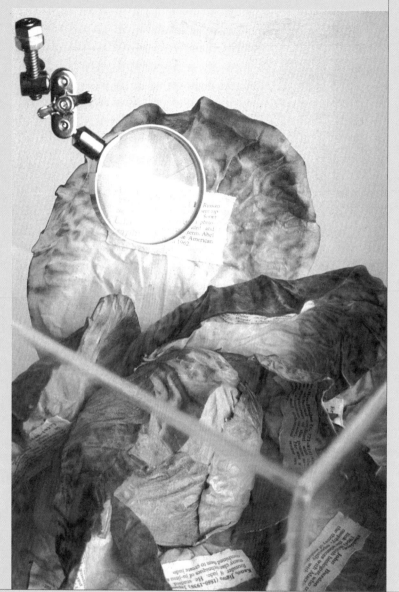

**JODY CULKIN
MEIGHAN GALE
MEGHAN GERETY
DAVID GILMORE
WAYNE GONZALES
DANNY GOODWIN
SARAH VANDERLIP
ANTON VIDOKLE**

This exhibition was styled rather than curated, with an emphasis on the complexity of the work rather than the curator's ideas. Using diverse approaches to subject matter and materials, this group of emerging artists was chosen as representative of work to be exhibited in the future at our Brooklyn space.

Jody Culkin (see page 8)

Since exhibiting with Momenta, Meighan Gale's work has been exhibited at Chamber 8, The Alternative Museum, Serge Sorokko Gallery, NYC and Rotunda Gallery, Brooklyn, NY.

Following the *Inaugural Exhibition* Meghan Gerety has exhibited her work in numerous shows including *Yes, No or Don't Know*, Andrew Kreps Gallery, NYC, *Fear Inflator*, GreeneNaftali Gallery, NYC, Lauren Wittels Gallery, NYC, and a two-person exhibition at 407 Gallery, NYC.

ANTON VIDOKLE, *Nostalgia*, detail, 1995, mixed media

David Gilmore (see page 11)

Since exhibiting at Momenta, Wayne Gonzales has exhibited with Mary Boone Gallery (project room), and had solo exhibitions at Tate Gallery, NYC, Derek Eller Gallery, NYC and Lauren Wittels Gallery, NYC. He has also exhibited in numerous group exhibitions, including *Brite Magic* at the Islip Museum in East Islip, NY.

Since this exhibit, Danny Goodwin's work has been included in exhibitions at the Brooklyn Museumof Art, Brooklyn, NY, Proposition Gallery, Belfast, Ireland, Parts Gallery in Minneapolis, MN, and a solo exhibition at Art Resources Transfer, Inc., NYC.

Following the *Inaugural Exhibition,* Sarah Vanderlip has had solo shows at XL/Xavier LaBoulbenne and at White Columns, NYC. Group exhibitions include *Still Gone (On the Persistence of Absence),* E.S. Vandam, NYC, *The Gaze*(see page 39), Momenta Art, Brooklyn, NY, and *Romper Room,* Thread Waxing Space, NYC.

Following this exhibition, Anton Vidokle has participated in numerous exhibitions including The Gramercy Art Fair (with Momenta Art), Deven Golden Fine Arts, NYC, and *Nobodies Home,* Momenta Art, Brooklyn, NY.

DANNY GOODWIN, *35mm SLR Pistol,* and *Telephone Bomb,* 1995, c-prints (top)

ANTON VIDOKLE, *Nostalgia,* and *Illustrations to Flaubert,* 1995, mixed media
WAYNE GONZALES, *Pink Face Painting,* 1995, acrylic on canvas (bottom)

JODY CULKIN

Jody Culkin's sculptures made from knitted steel wool, fabric, and welded steel combine threat and humor to create a gothic world of repressed desire. With titles like *Ethical Work*, *Moderation*, and *Let's Be Friends*, these cartoonish yet meticulous objects possess a faux utilitarianism, accentuating their irony. In *Shelf*, several sewn sacks resembling brightly colored body parts, severed and decorated, are displayed like candy or children's toys. She deliberately undermines her own sophisticated craftsmanship with quirky references to the domestic. The resultant objects appear to be tools of plots which continuously turn on themselves, creating a self-destructive comedy of errors.

Following this exhibition Culkin participated in numerous exhibitions including: *Urban Mythology*, Bronx Museum of Art, NYC, *Welded Sculptures*, Neuberger Museum, Purchase, NY, *La Coscienza Luccicante*, Comune di Roma Palazzo delle Esposizioni, Rome, Italy, and *The Model Home*, PS1 Museum at the Clocktower, NYC.

MIGUEL VENTURA

"Oh New Doctor! Can you extirpate this new tumor which is my tongue? And the new therapies, the new medications? Where are they?"

Miguel Ventura's installation, entitled *Cantonese Primer*, consists of over 30 toddlers' tee-shirts with multi-lingual slogans and laminated text in various languages, including Spanish, Swahili, German, and

obsessive and obscure nature of the artist's self-imposed systems manifests itself in a gallows humor of enforced identities.

Ventura's numerous solo exhibitions include *New Monuments to the Enemies Within*, Galeria Arte Contemporaneo, Mexico City, and *Miguel Ventura: Drawings*, Museum of Modern Art,

English. This strange hybrid-language is a complex system referencing educational pamphlets used by the far right and the far left. These slogans, familiar and perverse, contain an insular logic. The didactic imperatives combined with the children's clothing create a sense of powerlessness while the

Mexico City. Following his exhibition at Momenta, Ventura has participated in numerous exhibitions, including Jack Tilton Gallery, NYC, Cristinerose Gallery, NYC, and *Cambio*, curated by Kenny Schachter, NYC.

CHIN OPERATED BY ROD

JULIE MELTON

Julie Melton's series of drawings, entitled *Honey Pot, Check Yourself,* and *The Mother-fucker Everyone is Talking About,* obsessively expose and fragment incidents both spectacular and mundane, combining to create verbose and witty outbreaks unleashing unpredictable chain reactions. Her text and images, appropriated from conversations on subway platforms, wrestling magazines, opera, and children's science books, exist in a non-linear world where time swallows its tail and viewers follow.

Julie Melton received a BA and a BFA from East Carolina University, Greenville, NC, and an MFA from Tyler School of Art, Philadelphia, PA. Julie Melton's exhibition credits include The Drawing Center, NYC, and *The Art of Self Defense and Revenge,* Momenta Art, NYC. Since this exhibition Melton has produced numerous artist books, including *All or None, How to Recognize Him,* and *The Perfect Woman.* She has also designed original sets for plays, including *Moe Green Gets It In the Eye* and *The Coyote Bleeds,* NYC.

DAVID GILMORE

"The swallow was a symbol for gay sailors; a swallow tattoo was the unsmudgable mark. If you light a cigarette from a candle (legend has it), a sailor drowns."

David Gilmore's installation of sculpture, photographs, and sound, weave legend, superstition, and modern myth into an urgent narrative; the struggle between a failing body and a thriving mind. Tales of home remedies, suffering soldiers, *The War of The Worlds*, and etherized patients oscillate between humor and despair.

David Gilmore died of AIDS one week before the opening of this exhibition. He was twenty-seven years old.

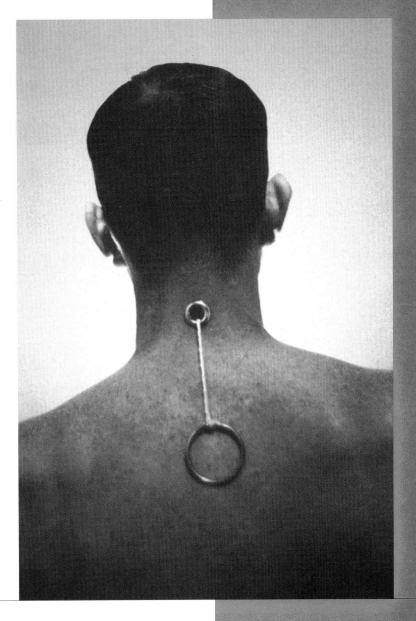

LISA ALBERTS
JOEY S. KÖTTING
ERIC HEIST
ANTHONY VITI

An examination of work that combines performance and painting, broadening the definition of figuration through reference to incidents outside the viewer's immediate field of vision. These offscreen performances employ unusual mediums such as mother's milk, a Lakers game, sugar, blood, and iodine. The abstractions appear embedded with information, almost archeological in nature.

Among Lisa Albert's exhibition credits are project room, Dooley Le Cappelaine, NYC, *Dirty Ornament,* Rotunda Gallery, Brooklyn, NY, and *Futura Book Collection,* Air de Paris, Nice, France.

ERIC HEIST, *Untitled* (detail), 1994, sugar, ink, polymer on linen (left)

JOEY S. KÖTTING, *Sunbathing with Sleeves Rolled Up*, 1995, gum bichromate, bulls blood on canvas (right)

After this exhibition Eric Heist participated in numerous shows, including P.S.1 Contemporary Art Center the Clocktower Galleries, NYC, Brooklyn Museum of Art, Brooklyn, NY, Larry Becker, Philadelphia, PA, and Feed, Brooklyn, NY.

Since this exhibition Joey S. Kötting has exhibited his work extensively. Selected exhibitions include Galeria Graca, Lisbon, Portugal, White Columns, NYC, Gallery Yvonne Lambert, Paris, France, and a two-person exhibition at Pace Wildenstein MacGill, NYC.

Following this show Anthony Viti's selected exhibitions include solo exhibitions at Deven Golden Fine Arts, NYC, Harnett Gallery, University of Rochester, NY, and group exhibitions at E.S. Vandam, and PPOW, NYC.

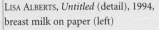

LISA ALBERTS, *Untitled* (detail), 1994, breast milk on paper (left)

ANTHONY VITI, *Trickle Drops*, 1994, human blood, urine, semen, charcoal and oil on wood panel (right)

GOTCHA!

SCOTT GALLOWAY
JUSTIN JAY
CHAS KRIDER
JULIE LANGSAM
MIKE MILLS
ODILI DONALD ODITA
OLU OGUIBE
CALVIN REID
FRITZ WELCH
DIRK WESTPHAL

Curated by Odili Donald Odita
Catalog Available

What is another name given to time when it is compacted so densely that it connotes only death? One calls this a picture. This is a show about pictures. *Gotcha!* specifically addresses pictures as the accumulative weight of time gone flat, focusing on the victim status we attain in relation to pictures as its subject and its viewer.

Think snapshots – random shots taken with a camera for the purpose of capturing a particular moment as a picture. This moment becomes instant forever. Now think yourself caught in that snap. Flash – gotcha! Frozen in time as the proxy of desire's victim. One is left to exist as a slice of reality marking time for those who were there to witness the spectacular moment and for those who would like to retain its image.

Installation view (from left to right)
ODILI DONALD ODITA, *Divine Brown, Communication Breakdown*, 1995, mixed media. FRITZ WELCH, *Liars vs. Truth, Tacky Souvenir*, and *Two-Sound Siren*, 1995, t-shirt, acrylic transfer, xerox transfer

Our bodies are commodities we consume in this area of display. Click, FLASH!... hardened like a diamond but without the wait, anonymousness and incongruity become our nature. We wait passively for that special someone to take us home and give us our name. "This person in the picture smiling with the hat, I'll call him...and that woman with the black dress, I'll call her..." It does not matter what nor who, it is the picture that counts here. It is the picture that will be here after we are gone.
—*Odili Donald Odita*

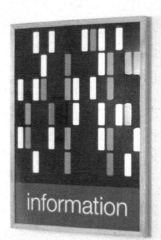

CALVIN REID, *Public Relations,* 1995, pen and ink on paper (top)

MIKE MILLS, *Cinema, Information, Science,* 1995, bubble jet print (bottom)

MARY ELLEN CARROLL

Mary Ellen Carroll's work links the boundaries of language and architecture. She examines the cultural/linguistic construction of American identity and the notion of the melting pot.

Using a text by St. John de Crevecoeur, an early U.S. immigrant, Carroll has taken each word back to its etymological root and printed this on an eight by ten foot sheet of paper. This has the effect of a reconstruction of Babel. The question becomes that of the reestablishment of an historical identity through language. The collective identity is distilled to its uncertain historical uniqueness. This elimination of the melting pot reduces the collective to its fragments, or back to the "individual." The paradox is "individualism" as the hallmark of the American identity and the "silent majority's" desire to be confined by the comfort of consensus as being an American.

Mary Ellen Carroll is a graduate of the University of Colorado and the Art Institute of Chicago. Her work has been exhibited at Frederieke Taylor/TZ'Art, NYC, The Palmer Museum, PA and the Stuttgart Stadt Galerie, Germany. Following her exhibition at Momenta, Carroll has exhibited with Galerie Hubert Winter in Berlin and Vienna, and Elizabeth Harris Gallery, NYC.

ROBERT BLANCHON

Robert Blanchon's wall installation of over 100 sepia prints (a blueprint-like process), in a wide range of sizes, of advertisements from gay periodicals, entitled *Untitled (1979-1981, (1995))*. The magazines from which Blanchon derived his imagery all pre-date AIDS. The ads consist of bizarre merchandise, including products such as a chest wig, cream to keep an erection for over seven hours, a how-to book on sex during hypnosis, and a picture of Michelangelo's David holding a bottle of poppers (amyl nitrate). Although several of these products

positive films and continually replenish the images, proposing responsibilities of conservation beyond the traditional realm of collecting. The decision not to keep the work active would be to allow a period of history to disappear. This device is designed with the role of collector as keeper of the memory of a time few remember.

Robert Blanchon was a graduate of the School of the Art Institute of Chicago and exhibited at the Randolph Street Gallery, Chicago, IL., White Columns, NYC, and

remain on the market to some extent, most are historical artifacts from the height of the sexual revolution for gay men (and others). The prints, simply map-tacked to the wall, salon style, will eventually fade, like blueprints, into oblivion. Anyone interested in obtaining this work must purchase the

University of California, Irvine, CA. Following his exhibition at Momenta, Blanchon exhibited with Marc Foxx, Santa Monica, CA, and the Los Angeles Center for Photographic Studies, Los Angeles, CA.

Robert Blanchon died of AIDS in 1999.

WILLIAM ALLEN

William Allen's enamel paintings counter-balance American folk art with hypertext. Here narrative is imputed onto steel, and so too are certain notions about the intel-lectual, psychological and metonymic courses a poem or story should run. The words chosen make startling or strange connections. Their hand-painted quality is subverted by their pristine surfaces, just as the sounds of words are subverted by their etymologies.

A poet and painter, Allen is the author of several books including *Sevastopol: On Photographs of War* (Xenos Press), 1997, and *The Man on the Moon* (NYU/Persea Presses, 1987). Recent poems have appeared in *Chelsea Magazine, Callaloo,*

SPIRITUS MUNDI
GUDRUN ENSSLIN
FONTAINEBLEAU

The American Voice, Global City Review, and Poetry East. Allen has exhibited art-work and poetry in *Committed to Print* at the MOMA, and in a two-person exhibi-tion (with Barbara Westermann) at Williams College in Williamstown, MA.

BARBARA WESTERMANN

Barbara Westermann uses plaster and epoxy to explore relationships among signage, the occult, and contemporary art-making practices. Her sculptures operate as a conceptual alphabet based on medieval signs that originated in pharmacology, alchemy, and architecture. These morphed characters have a strange domestic quality. Their porcelain veneer turns these quasi-scientific hieroglyphs into a kind of bathtub chemistry that reexamines constructivist impulses while alluding to real aspects of everyday life.

Westermann has exhibited her work extensively, including at Freiburg Museum of Contemporary Art in Germany, and in a solo exhibition at La Jolla Museum of Contemporary Art, CA. After her exhibition at Momenta, Westermann exhibited her work at Holly Solomon Gallery, NYC, Newport Art Museum, Newport, RI, Brooklyn Museum of Art, Brooklyn, NY, and in a two-person exhibition(with William Allen) at Williams College, Williamstown, MA.

MARSHA PELS

Marsha Pels's installation was inspired by her visit to Botswana, Africa, and contains a 12' kayak covered with white goose wings, dismembered wax doll appendages, and encaustic organic forms splayed along its central axis. This disturbing tableau also contains a female "child-doll" sporting a huge rubber dildo and blowing a horn. She hangs in space surveying the smaller bodies succumbed in the central ark, a grotesque exaggeration of Pels's earlier bronze asexual, archetypal putti. Pels employs the boat form metaphorically to conjure a body/landscape transgressing psychological and spatial boundaries while the doll, through material transformations from crystal and bronze, acts as a surrogate child. As a signifier of loss of innocence, Pels's "dolls" are aggressive but helpless – trapped by larger forces – be they nature or culture.

Since this exhibition, Pels has received a Fulbright Senior Scholarship to Germany and has been the Keynote Speaker at the International Conference (Glass Art Society) and Artist/Lecturer at the International Bunker Symposium in connection with a site-specific Holocaust memorial in Eden, Germany. She has also exhibited in numerous group shows including *The Theater of Cruelty*, Christinerose Gallery, NYC, and *Spring Show*, Connemara Nature Conservancy, Dallas, TX.

DONNA CZAPIGA

Donna Czapiga's complex paintings utilize renaissance glazing techniques and cartoonish enamel abstractions, creating a dichotomy of styles. Lush, moody surfaces pulsate between lighter gestural marks, creating continuous shifts of allusion from carefully layered landscapes to abrupt figuration. The wood panels the artist utilizes as supports for exquisitely prepared grounds create an "objectness" accentuated by carefully considered edges - paradoxical to the thin varnished layers of pigment that seem to be part liquid, part vapor. This viscous surface has the appearance of tainted honey or milk and seems virtually edible.

Czapiga lives and works in Philadelphia and received a BA from the University of Delaware. Following her exhibit at Momenta, selected exhibitions include Fleisher Art Memorial, Philadelphia, PA, Larry Becker Contemporary Art, Philadelphia, PA, Locks Gallery, Philadelphia, PA, and the University of Delaware, Newark, DE.

JOSH SINGER

Joshua Singer's paintings are constructed from paints derived from industrial pigments. Some of these pigments are commonly used in the automotive and plastics industry; one is used in the manufacture of the coatings of NATO warplanes. Singer's apparently minimalist work alludes to the cultural baggage of his chosen materials, while implicating the viewer through mirror-like painted surfaces achieved using traditionally-based glazing and varnishing techniques.

Shown in combination with the paintings, Singer's video work explores the formal and moral conventions of narrative construction through his manipulation of appropriated cinema, "handmade" images, and found audio.

Joshua Singer is a graduate of Hampshire College and Hunter College in New York and has exhibited at Julian Pretto Gallery, NYC and White Columns, NYC. Following his exhibition at Momenta, Singer has screened work at various venues including Brooklyn Museum of Art, Brooklyn, NY, Gavin Brown Enterprise, NYC, and the Worldwide Video Festival, Amsterdam, The Netherlands.

STEPHEN ANTONSON

Stephen Antonson examines public space and public memory with his *Untitled* installation exhibited at Momenta. Antonson creates a drop ceiling of backlit, frosted plexiglas tiles, silk-screened with an aerial view of plane crash wreckage from a photograph printed in the *New York Times*. Like Warhol's disaster series, this cold yet emotionally charged image blurs distinctions between media and art while emphasizing the power of an image to create a public memory. The ceiling tiles, when seen individually, appear as abstract patterns. These decorative crash fragments create an unsettling atmosphere which is intensified by the sound of static emanating from speakers set into the ceiling.

Antonson is a graduate of Hunter College in New York and Carnegie Mellon University, College of Fine Arts in Pittsburgh, PA. Following his exhibition at Momenta, Antonson has participated in numerous group exhibitions, including P.S.1 Contemporary Art Center The Clocktower Galleries, Swiss Institute, NYC, Elizabeth Harris Gallery, NYC, and White Columns, NYC. He has also had a two-person exhibition at Lauren Wittels Gallery, NYC, and a solo exhibition at Elizabeth Harris Gallery, NYC.

LISELOT VAN DER HEIJDEN

Liselot van der Heijden's installation, entitled *Nature,* uses projected video stills to examine the consumption of "the natural." A visit to a national park reveals events in parking lots where tourists become papparazzi of the "wild." The camera becomes a gun substitute; a means of capture/objectification. This allows for the ultimate relaxation for the hardcore vacationing

hysteric mechanisms of human culture than the essential truths of the subjects they intend to convey. With a sense of humor and irony, van der Heijden shifts the gaze from the spectacle and rests it on the spectator.

Liselot van der Heijden is a graduate of Cooper Union For the Advancement of Science And Art, and is a participant in the traveling exhibition *Monumental Propaganda*, organized by Komar and

consumer. The vacation from the "civilized world" is broken down into a series of climactic moments of purchase and capture.

These images of wild animals obsessively being photographed, documented, and videotaped ultimately reveal more about the

Melamid. Following her exhibition at Momenta, Liselot van der Heijden exhibited her work and screened her videos at numerous venues, including *The New York Video Festival*, NYC, Brooklyn Museumof Art, Brooklyn, NY, Kunstmuseum, Milwaukee, WI, and Artists Space, NYC.

ROBERT BOYD

Robert Boyd's sculptures address societal constructs of identity versus individual constructs of desire and homosexuality. His piece, entitled *Cofradia* (Spanish for brotherhood), is made of thirty-one suspended silver and white conical caps. Derived from the *corozas* placed upon the heads of the accused during the Spanish Inquisition, the caps were shortly thereafter transformed into ritualistic costumes adorning the flagellants during the procession of Holy Week. They have come down to us in history as dunce caps and more recently as part of the uniforms of Klansmen. Boyd uses this conflated history to reflect upon the spectacle of desire and the underlying homoeroticism of initiates into all-male groups.

Boyd also exhibited *Tumult*, a writhing phallic landscape cast in aluminum, and *Cage*, a large steel bird cage containing fragile blown glass drops filled with water, suspended over a mirror pool. This image is derived from 17th century portrait painting, in which a cage with an open door symbolizes the death of the person portrayed.

Robert Boyd studied at Tyler School of Art, Philadelphia, PA, and Cooper Union For the Advancement of Science And Art, NYC. He has exhibited his work at Artists Space and Black and Herron Space, NYC. Following his exhibition at Momenta, Boyd has exhibited at Cristinerose Gallery, NYC, and Elga Wimmer Gallery, NYC. He has also curated several exhibitions, including *Contact* at Jack Tilton Gallery, NYC.

GORDON FREMAUX
YAEL KANAREK
MATTHEW FREEDMAN
JULIA PEPPITO
RANDY WRAY

These artists weave references from American folk art, popular culture and art history to create images which challenge notions of beauty. Using non-traditional materials they defy conventional approaches to painting and sculpture.

"I paint figures which personify different levels of consciousness in a weird utopian world aware of the presence of monstrosity."
Gordon Fremaux

In Gordon Fremaux's painting *Supertramp*, a fakir holding birds' nests sits cross-legged in midtown Manhattan, sworn not to lower his hands until birds nest in them. He is treated as just another bizarre spectacle on the streets of New York by those passing by.

Yael Kanarek's *Untitled* paintings *(from the Love Letters From the World of Awe Series)* use acrylic, candy sprinkles and papier-mâché to question the power of art as a signifier of the sublime. The texts from this series are letters from an alienated traveler searching through an artificial landscape for the experience of awe. Kanarek's cartoon bombs, paper snow flakes, demonic Dr. Seuss characters, and birds flying in a smiley face formation pull every cheap trick in the sublime, romantic, painted, landscape book, all to no avail. Such desperation emphasizes the limitations of art, contrasted with the sincere desire to transcend those limitations.

"*The figures in my installations are crude and rough, almost not there, though present in great numbers. The significance of each individual piece is diminished in a crowd, but their collective presence is increased.*"
Matthew Freedman

Matthew Freedman's air-dried clay figures are hastily hand-molded and painted in a way which speaks of urgency and frailty. These wounded and slovenly figures are humorous on an individual basis, but collectively their frailties become grotesque and menacing.

Julia Peppito's *Untitled* installation, constructed of ashtrays, fishing bait, electrical tape, glitter, and fabric, appears as both a child's dream fort and a set from a David Cronenberg film. Glittering yet grotesque sexual members protrude and recede in a stuffed star which doubles as an infant toy; squishy bubbles are both squeeze toys and boils; and only after closer examination does the viewer recognize that receding eyes are everywhere.

In Randy Wray's paintings the artist applies craft-making techniques such as paint-by-numbers and macramé to create complex abstractions. Wray makes no distinctions between "appropriate" and "inappropriate" materials. Free to utilize images and objects reflective of his personal experiences and tastes, his paintings confound categorization. They are both abstract and representational, decorative and grotesque.

RANDY WRAY, *Mill*, 1996, mixed media (facing page, top left)

JULIA PEPPITO, *Bug*, 1996, mixed media (facing page top right)

MATTHEW FREEDMAN, *Untitled*, 1996, clay, acrylic (facing page, bottom)

GORDON FREMAUX, *Supertramp*, 1996, acrylic on canvas (top)

YAEL KANAREK, *The Point of No Return*, 1996, mixed media (bottom)

INSIDE/OUT

JENNIFER BOLANDE
LISA HEIN
CANNON HUDSON
JAMES MILLS
ROXY PAINE
WILLIAM SCHUCK

The artists participating in the exhibition *Inside/Out* use various mediums to examine architecture's physical and mental constructs. Through depicted and real spaces they draw distinctions between interior versus exterior, as well as public versus private space.

JAMES MILLS, *For Free*, 1996, sign (above)

LISA HEIN, *Salon*, 1996, displaced gallery closet, existing fuse boxes, picture lights (right)

Roxy Paine, *Studio*, 1996, steel and electronics (left)

Jennifer Bolande, *Stacks* (detail), 1995, C-prints on aluminum (above)

Jennifer Bolande's *Untitled* Iris prints are composites operating like cinematic jump cuts. They are disjointed narratives of optical information paths from object to subject; the interior of an eyeball to a landscape. These paths, both quiet and direct, connect the nature of physical space to the mental process of the viewer.

Lisa Hein zeroes in on Momenta Art's architectural anomaly: a wedge-shaped closet housing the building's electrical service. Her site-specific installation displaces the focus of exhibition from the pristine walls to the system sustaining it.

Cannon Hudson's recent paintings from the *Untitled (stations)* series reference work sta-tions, conversation pits, and automobile inte-riors. Graphic paint application abstracts the image. These stations float, ungrounded, becoming a mental landscape of boundaries and symbols for operating in physical space.

James Mills's sign attached to the exterior of the gallery resembles a real estate sign reading *For Free*. This humorous yet poignant word play subverts commodifica-tion and signs of gentrification evident in the neighborhood of Williamsburg. Similarly, Mills's series of scale models examines issues of public versus private property, value and obsolescence.

Roxy Paine transforms his studio into a diorama by installing a periscope down into the gallery, which peers into his studio located above Momenta Art. Public versus private space is accentuated through sur-veillance, voyeurism, and exhibitionism. William Schuck creates a vinyl model, with dimensions identical to several walls in the gallery, on the roof of the building housing Momenta Art. Throughout a three-week period prior to the opening of the exhibi-tion, Schuck continuously coated the replica walls with polyurethane. This coating process trapped airborne debris, leaving a record of time and space which was then installed in the gallery for the duration of the exhibition.

JACKIE CHANG

Jackie Chang's *Art Created by the Artist Made by Someone Else* is a collection of works designed by the artist but made by manufacturers located around Momenta Art in Williamsburg, Brooklyn. The exhibition includes a venting duct made by a sheet metal fabricator and painted at an auto body shop, a large plastic wall cover made to specifications by a plastic furniture covering shop, and 10-foot zippers created by the zipper manufacturer next door to the gallery. Each piece is identified with a "j. chang made in the U.S.A." cloth label made by Triangle Labels in Williamsburg. The exhibition examines the artist as maker, as well as the complex partnership between artists, galleries and the existing neighborhood in a fast-growing artist community.

Jackie Chang received an MFA from The School of the Art Institute of Chicago. Selected exhibitions include Rotunda Gallery, Brooklyn, NY, Art in General, NYC and Peter Miller Gallery, Chicago, IL. Since her exhibition at Momenta, Chang has created public works for the Public Art Fund, NYC, the Metropolitan Transit Authority, NYC, and the Brooklyn Public Library, Brooklyn, NY.

j. chang
made in
U.S.A.

JESSE'S PLASTIC COVERS

SARAH VOGWILL

Sarah Vogwill's installation, *Sentimental Education,* works through the loss of representations invested with a 19th century sentimental aesthetic. A series of glass shelves on decorative brackets presents arrangements of mementos, found objects, and photographs embodying the melancholic tone of this work. Here *La Vie Interieur* is defended as the refuge of emotional introspection against the encroaching metropolis. But the pleasures of melancholy run up against the threat of public repression. "*Don't cry,*" say the Narcissus-like mirrors. The viewer is nonetheless invited to participate: offered a seat in *Uncle Selby's Chair* near a plant sobbing shrilly; and finally, a calling card, with the words "*What's it like to know I've seen your tears.*"

Sarah Vogwill is a graduate of California Institute of the Arts and attended the Whitney Independent Study Program in New York. Selected exhibitions include the Urban Institute of Contemporary Art, Grand Rapids, MI, YYZ, Toronto, and the Atlanta Arts Festival (with REPOhistory).

LESLIE BRACK

Leslie Brack's paintings based on female tabloid celebrities examine the thin line between glamour and vulgarity while exposing stereotypes perpetuated by the celebrity machine. Brack combines color schemes borrowed from fashion magazines with texts such as *Actress Girlfriend, Sometime Actress*, or *Sitcom Blonde*. These headlines, suspended from their sources, appear as part insult,

embarrassingly vulgar and yet incongruous on this afternoon's L.A. red carpet." The discomfort that lies behind American celebrity culture informs this body of work.

Leslie Brack received an MFA from The School of the Art Institute of Chicago, and a BA at Evergreen State College, WA. Following her exhibition at Momenta,

part sexual innuendo. As Brack explains, "The overall effect of this work is similar to seeing *NYPD Blue's* Sharon Lawrence on Emmy night. Sharon wore a shimmery floor-length Chanel gown straight from today's top magazines. Unfortunately, what looked so great in yesterday's *Vogue* looks

Brack has participated in numerous exhibitions including (two-person show) PS122, NYC, *Encyclopedia 1999*, Turner & Runyon Gallery, Dallas, TX, and solo exhibitions at Yearsley Spring Gallery, Philadelphia, PA, Hofstra University, NY, and a project room at Galerie Jousse Seguin in Paris, France.

AUNRICO GATSON

Aunrico Gatson's video sculptures reference puritanical design while exposing the origins of stereotypes in American society. These works appear initially as simple, elegantly crafted black and white structures, yet the maniacal, muffled soundtrack hints at monstrous characters contained within. The viewer is forced to interact with the objects in order to witness the videos, which utilize images such as the blackfaced minstrel, reversed, as a "given" cultural image. This work tempers an emotive terrain with a simple, formal approach to black and white. As the artist quietly asserts, *"I am interested in these colors both formally and symbolically."*

Aunrico Gatson received an MFA from Yale School of Art and a BA from Bethel College, St. Paul, MN. Following his exhibition at Momenta, Gatson participated in numerous exhibitions, including Brooklyn Museum of Art, Brooklyn, NY, *Hybro Video*, Exit Art, NYC, and solo exhibitions at Pierogi 2000, Brooklyn, NY, and Ronald Feldman Fine Arts, NYC. He was an Artist in Residence at Franconia Sculpture Park, St. Paul, MN.

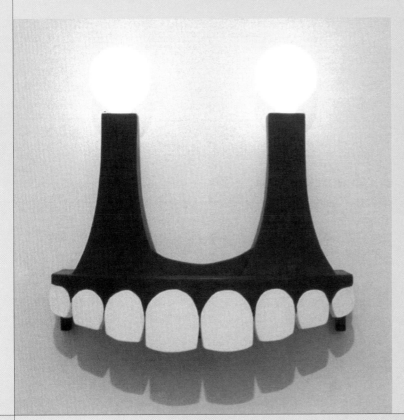

TORU HAYASHI

Toru Hayashi's installation made with empty shoes, stockings, and cast wax fists examines issues of sexuality and discrimination while leaving the viewer with a disturbing sense of absence. The wall texts stating *20% off* and *50% off* are strangely humorous next to the deflated figures. These figurative sculptures appear like empty clothes racks, causing the viewer to question the way our society values individuals.

Toru Hayashi is a graduate of Hokkaido University in Sapporo, Japan. He has exhibited his work at the Bronx Museum *Artist in the Marketplace* exhibition. Since his exhibition at Momenta he has exhibited his work and performed at Rotunda Gallery, Brooklyn, NY, *First Look*, Down-town Arts Festival, NYC, and TAKA, NYC.

ELANA HERZOG

Elana Herzog uses familiar domestic materials to imply mutation and growth or decay. These sewn elastic and fabric pieces are part infants' clothing and part diseased decoration. The tawdry and garish nature of the materials is evocative and playfully sculptural, traversing limits of attraction and repulsion and challenging our experience of beauty as an indicator of taste.

Elana Herzog received an MFA from SUNY, Alfred, NY, and a BA from Bennington College, VT. Following her exhibition at Momenta, Herzog has exhibited at Brooklyn Museum of Art, Brooklyn, NY, Arti Et Amicitiae, Amsterdam, The Netherlands. She has had solo shows at PPOW Gallery, NYC, ArtNation Projects, Inc., NYC, and Mercer Union, Toronto, Canada.

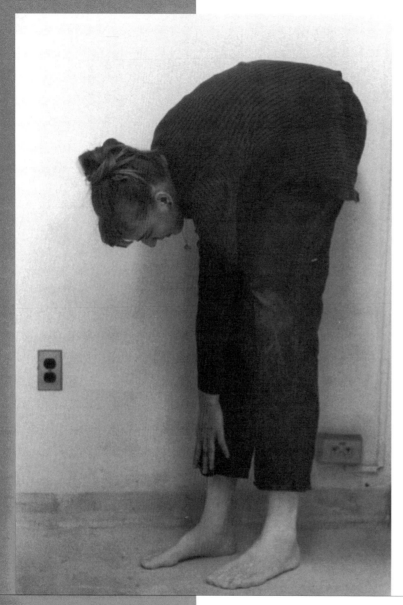

SUE DE BEER

Sue de Beer uses staged videos, photographs, and performances to examine how the media affects our perception of the natural. Using puns and tasteless jokes as unlikely inspirations, she alludes to events that are simultaneously disastrous and banal. Her use of abject props emphasizes her perversely quixotic attempts to defy the laws of physics and social convention. Her performance, entitled *Endurance*, features exercise videos with the artist and her partner on a sofa, prosthetically joined at the lips.

Sue de Beer received a BA from Parsons School of Design and an MFA from Columbia University. Following her exhibition at Momenta, de Beer has exhibited her work at numerous venues, including Brooklyn Museum of Art, Brooklyn, NY, Jack Tilton Gallery, NYC, *Video Library*, David Zwirner Gallery, NYC, Apex Art, NYC, the project room at Galerie Jousse Seguin, Paris, France, and a solo exhibition at Deitch Projects, NYC.

KRISTIN LUCAS

Kristin Lucas's video sculptures debate the pros and cons of "interactivity" and the pervasiveness of media as culture. The artist positions herself as both spectator and media spectacle in scripted performances; she uses video to record and add dimension to the complexity of her position as a woman in a technocratic society. The sculptural elements of her installa-

Kristin Lucas received a BA from Cooper Union for Advancement of Science and Art. Her videos have been screened in *The Young and the Restless* exhibit at the Museum of Modern Art, NYC. Following her exhibition at Momenta, Lucas exhibited with numerous venues, including Artists Space, NYC, Dia Center for the Arts, NYC, P.S.1 Contemporary Art

tions are adaptations of household tools and toys, gutted and juiced-up with an assortment of electronic components. In her performance at Momenta, Lucas presides as video jockey *Lo$$Vegas*, mixing sound bites from prerecorded VHS tapes with a live camera feed.

Center, Long Island City, NY, and Jack Tilton Gallery, NYC. Her work was included in the 1997 *Whitney Biennial*, NYC.

THE GAZE

JANET BIGGS
KATHE BURKHART
NICOLE EISENMAN
MARIA ELENA GONZALEZ
LAURE LEBER
LORRAINE O'GRADY
JOCELYN TAYLOR
SARAH VANDERLIP
KARA WALKER
AMANDA WILLIAMSON

Catalog Available

The artists included in the exhibition entitled *The Gaze* are interested in redefining the way women look at themselves and each other. "The gaze" has been defined as male property – a tool to transform the power of female sexuality into a malleable reflection of male desire. How men look at women has been examined extensively, while the way that women perceive themselves as well as other women has been a neglected subject.

The exhibition attempts to give an historical context to these contemporary female artists by examining their work in relation to the history of feminist theory. Wall text containing quotes from such critical theorists as Laura Mulvey and Mary Ann

Doane gives a context to the work that is often ignored but always present.

Janet Biggs's photographs and videos of young girls learning to ride horseback and tread water imply sexuality through camera placement in relation to the subject, yet the activities in which they participate are typical of children their age. As they learn to use their bodies to negotiate physical space, they simultaneously learn that they are "to be watched."

Kathe Burkhart's painting *Slit* subverts male language and mass media representation of the female while commenting on female discomfort with the body. The image of Elizabeth Taylor appears as both victim and martyr as she recovers from a plastic surgery operation.

Installation view with the work (from left to right) of MARIA ELENA GONZALEZ, KATHE BURKHART, SARAH VANDERLIP, LAURE LEBER

Lorraine O'Grady's four photos titled *The Gaze* examine possibilities of reclaiming black subjectivity, particularly in the case of the black female. The images work as collapsed diptychs. The outer image operates as a mask of disdain while the inner image is that of the same person with a slight yet knowing smile, reminding both viewer and subject of the possibility of subjectivity.

Jocelyn Taylor's *Jocelyn in Chair, Eyeballs in Bowl* literalizes the internalization of the gaze in this two-channel video work as the artist is depicted from behind, seated, reaching from one monitor to another, appearing to take eyeballs from a bowl, one by one, and inserting them into her vagina.

Nicole Eisenman's untitled collage of cover girls covered in the artist's lipstick prints subverts the male gaze and notions of the fetishized female by exposing lesbian desire and emphasizing the unattainability of cultural notions of beauty.

Maria Elena Gonzalez's sculpture *Untitled (Hamper)* uses a domestic object as a means to question notions of identity. The reflection in the mirror placed on the top of the piece is disrupted by a phallic object that is both attractive and repulsive. This Lacanian reconstruction of the everyday object forces the viewer's reflection both literally and metaphorically.

Laure Leber's sexually charged portraits subvert pornographic imagery by approaching photography in a way that is stylized yet journalistic. The casual and realistic details of the settings for these portraits combined with an exacting lighting and composition causes her work to drift somewhere between the real and the staged.

Sarah Vanderlip's video stills of herself dressed in blow-up doll costume confront viewers with their fears of sexuality as this animated sex toy resembles a combination life-size children's doll and masturbation device.

Kara Walker's disturbing silhouettes ask the viewer to examine the historic representation of the black female as "exotic seductress." These images express despair and conquest as women are both desired and despised by their "masters."

Amanda Williamson combines suggestive yet not explicit female nude photos with grease pencil tracings from pornographic magazines. This strange hybrid questions notions of the erotic as well as differences in the nature of the female and the male gaze.

JANET BIGGS, *Amanda On Top, Twins Below*, 1997, C-print, laser disk, monitor (left)

NICOLE EISENMAN, *Untitled (kisses)*, 1996, lipstick and gouache on magazine page (bottom)

L. A. ANGELMAKER

L. A. Angelmaker's installation, entitled *Bad Penny: For Museum Purchase Only, January 1996, Part I of XII,* examines the way in which objects of art circulate through public and private institutions. The installation includes a display of objects that were deaccessioned from museum collections. In it, auction catalogs are presented on sculptural bases, each illustrating these objects. Also included is a

The artist provides information concering his most recent exhibition: *Sensaround,* Pamela Auchincloss Project Space, NYC, July 2-September 19, 1998. My last exhibition was a group show that explored the five senses. I exhibited a project entitled *Text: Thill, Robert, "MTV Looks For a Piece of the Art World," Flash Art (International) 30, no. 194 (May-June 1997): 50. Read by*

renaissance-style table loaned by a private antique dealer for the duration of the exhibition. The actual object and the illustrated objects are offered for sale back to the institutions that deaccessioned them through letters, printed on gallery stationery, displayed in the gallery. Responses from the museums are displayed as they are received.

James Traub. A closed magazine encased in plexiglas as speakers extend from the ceiling like spotlights and project a voice reading the *Flash Art* review toward the magazine. The audible text, which operates as a kind of "art-criticism-on-tape," is intended to illuminate the object, highlighting art writing as subject matter.

FRANCIS CAPE

Francis Cape exhibits two works which reference woodworking techniques from the turn of the century. Both pieces are based on window shutter designs that were manufactured circa 1860. *Lincoln Avenue* is based on actual shutters located in Brooklyn combined with a pattern from a book on woodworking from the turn of the century. Similarly, *Ravenscroft St.* is based on shutters from the artist's previous residence in London. Cape uses an English Victorian vernacular to question the anonymity of the artisan and the individuality of the contemporary artist. These quiet pieces are like uprooted domestic objects whose meaning has been transformed by their presence in a gallery setting. Although they reference minimalism, their highly-crafted, anti-manufactured quality add a level of humor and nostalgia which subverts the austerity of the gallery setting. Their domestic reference questions the distinction between the gallery and home, where "decorative objects" are created anonymously.

Francis Cape is a graduate of Goldsmiths College, University of London, and attended Skowhegan School of Painting and Sculpture. His work has been exhibited at Basilico Fine Arts, NYC, Steffany Martz, NYC, and Clove Gallery, London. Following his exhibition at Momenta, Cape has exhibited with Andrea Rosen Gallery, NYC, and has had solo exhibitions at Murray Guy, NYC and at The College of Saint Rose Art Gallery, Albany, NY.

SEONG CHUN

Seong Chun's obsessive sculptures, constructed from paper, crochet, and thread are embedded with almost subliminal text. Words are printed onto the surface of the paper, which is then painstakingly and elaborately stripped, joined, and folded to make "spools" of paper yarn. Chun employs texts such as Italo Calvino's *Invisible Cities* and Gaston Bachelard's *The Poetics of Space* to contemplate the infinite permutations of memory and ideas that challenge truths and actualities of past experiences.

The obsessiveness of these works seems to examine unaccountable time. They are an attempt to assign meaning and reason to many seemingly nonsensical fetishized moments hidden in the interiors of our routines.

Seong Chun is a graduate of Tyler School of Art and New York University. Following her exhibition at Momenta, Chun has exhibited her work in numerous exhibitions, including Weatherspoon Art Gallery, Greensboro, NC, Castle Gallery, New Rochelle, NY, and solo exhibitions at Esso Gallery, NYC, Byron Cohen Gallery, Kansas City, MO, the Brooklyn Public Library, Brooklyn, NY, and Elizabeth Harris Gallery, NYC.

ERIC WOLSKE

Eric Wolske presents a series of drawings which disturb perceived scale by oscillating between micro and macro. These drawings are made by piling several ink drops on top of one another on soaked paper. The complexity of the effects depends partially on chance, creating luminous spots of color on white fields. Wolske manipulates the images to resemble quasars and distant galaxies, or microscopic viruses and gene clusters.

Eric Wolske is a graduate of Hunter College in New York and has exhibited his work at Weatherspoon Art Gallery, Greensboro, NC, and The Drawing Center, NYC.

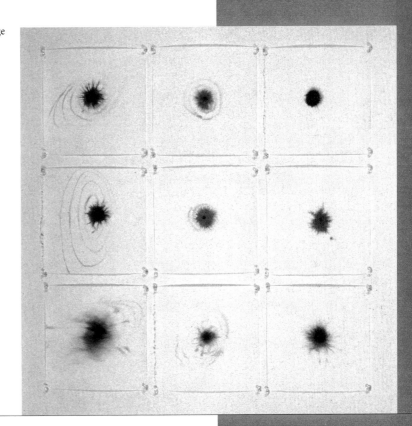

PETER SCOTT

Peter Scott's work intrudes into the safety of domestic settings while considering issues of class and privilege. This untitled installation appears at first to contain nothing but elegant wallpaper. Upon closer examination, images of police sketches of criminals emerge before the viewer. This work presents the American preoccupation with crime as well as our fascination with those who have transgressed the social order.

In re-presenting these drawings on the reverse of wallpaper, a surface which suggests comfort and familiarity, one's confidence in the distinctions between the world "out there" and one's private experience of it is called into question. Pattern and surface texture, usually functioning as decoration, alternately camouflage and reveal the perpetrators beneath, but never completely contain or obliterate them. The pleasantness of a mildly affluent room suggested by the satin walls is disquieted by the notion that they lack solidity, providing no safe borders between ourselves and the world at large.

Peter Scott is a graduate of the Rhode Island School of Design and attended the Rijksakadamie van Beeldende Kunsten in Amsterdam, The Netherlands. His work has been exhibited at White Columns, NYC, Galerie Rizzo, Paris, De Lege Ruimte, Brugge, Belgium, and Real Art Ways, Hartford, CT. Following his exhibition at Momenta, Scott has exhibited at *The Best Surprise is No Surprise*, Holiday Inn, NYC. He guest-curated an exhibition at Momenta titled *Nobodies Home* (see pages 64-65), and received a NYFA fellowship in sculpture.

KAREN YAMA

Karen Yama's work considers the construction of the social self through diverse photographic imagery. *Chop Shop Dragster* depicts miniature sculptures built from plastic car model kits. Model parts, carefully ordered in mass-produced packages, work as metaphors for the constituents of social identities. Set in a miniature simulated gallery constructed by

photographer from behind, cropped down to buttocks by the camera. While the officers' guns and billy clubs represent the power of the state, the images suggest that these policeman are themselves policed. Strapped into regulation belts, their personas can only be surmised.

Karen Yama received an MFA from the Rhode Island School of Design and a BA from the University of California, Davis.

the artist, the self is presented as artificial, styled for a world which asks that we be more palatable than real.

In *Even the Job is an Artificial Limb, (Fuzz Kits '96),* both police officers and actors in the role of police are stalked by the

Her work has been exhibited at Art in General and Artists Space, NYC. She has been granted residencies at The MacDowell Colony, Yaddo Corporation, the Fine Arts Work Center in Province-town, and the Marie Sharpe Walsh Foundation, NYC.

HOWARD SCHWARTZBERG

Howard Schwartzberg presents an untitled installation comprised of excerpts from separate but linked series of works. Central to this installation are two sculptural paintings which literally turn painting inside out to expose its constructs. These works appear as burlap sacks filled with paint. Their polished saturated surfaces contrast with the bulging burlap, which acts

Drawings from the *Product* series and the *Patient* series utilize Miracle Gro fertilizer, plastic bags and seeds. These works use word play and metaphor to speak of both a historical critique and a personal narrative.

Howard Schwartzberg attended Pratt Institute and Hunter College in New York. His work has been exhibited at Stux

as a repository for memory and personal histories while alluding to the historical baggage of painting. These filled containers are simultaneously cynical and nostalgic. As with all of Schwartzberg's work, they speak of decay and the potential for growth.

Gallery, NYC. Following his exhibition at Momenta he exhibited with Linda Kirkland Gallery, NYC, and Socrates Sculpture Park, Long Island City, NY. He also had a solo exhibition at the Silverstein Gallery, NYC.

DALE ANTHONY

Dale Anthony literalizes the painted surface by adding detritus from the studio floor in a pseudo-tromp l'oeil manner, through which he investigates the constructs of painting. These works, simultaneously cynical and sincere, operate as commentary alluding to the "death of painting" while attempting to reinvent a formal language of personal gestures. Created with throw-away materials, these mixed-media paintings imply an open-ended personal narrative. They pose questions about value and meaning, asking the viewer to complete the narrative based on clues carefully drawn from the rubbish heap.

Dale Anthony lives and works in New Zealand. He studied at Wellington Polytechnic and Elam Art School in New Zealand, and has exhibited his work at Peter McLeavey Gallery, NYC, and 450 Broadway Gallery, NYC.

ZVEZDANA ROGIC

Zvezdana Rogic's installation, *Out of Context: Moving Through the Zone of Separation,* consists of two sculpture projects: *Letters/Slova,* and *Vuko-mobile in New York.* Both works draw from the artist's experience as a Serbian in America, and are engaged in a discourse of identity formation in relation to contemporary international politics.

In *Letters/Slova,* letter forms of various materials hang about the gallery in clusters, forming words in two languages, English and Serbian (formerly, Serbo-Croatian). The words chosen form an uneasy linguistic constellation. No grouping amounts to a sentence. Rather, as linguistic connectors of divergent realms of meaning, the words function as tools of negotiation.

Vuko-mobile in New York, a collaboration with Steven Brower, explores public protest speech in Yugoslavia and its altered ramifications through transplantation into New York City. It can be seen as a personal extension of the democratic protest of the winter of 96/97 in Belgrade, Yugoslavia. On the gallery floor is a small replica of a vehicle that was used in the demonstrations as a mobile podium for protest speakers. The work mourns the loss of protest as it is pays homage to the ingenious design of this hybrid vehicle/stage.

Zvezdana Rogic received a BA from Cooper Union For the Advancement of Art and Science and attended the Whitney Independent Study Program, NYC. Her work has been exhibited at Chamber and White Columns, NYC. Following her exhibition at Momenta, Rogic had a solo exhibition at the Brooklyn Public Library, Brooklyn, NY.

CYNTHIA LOVETT

Cynthia Lovett's installation, entitled *Big Meetings,* combines a family history with elements of a collective past to explore the notion of a scapegoat and its accusers. The decaying wood of turned-over picnic tables and benches appears as ruins surrounded by wallprints of audience members at an unnamed event. These crowd images are derived from various source materials ranging from a lynching to a sports event. Central to the piece is a video of the artist's father relating a comical anecdote about his pet goat's inevitable sacrifice for the church's annual "big meeting." As the story is told it becomes more and more detached from its intimate context, viewers consider whether they are identifying with or objectifying this family.

Further, the nonlinear narratives of *Big Meetings* function as emblematic texts that multiply in meaning. They are recollections constructed both visually and orally to reveal potential correlations between the deeply personal experience and the collective one.

Cynthia Lovett received an MFA from Tyler School of Art, Philadelphia, PA, and a BFA from Howard University, Washington, DC. She participated in the P.S.1 Contemporary Art Center's National Studio program. Since her exhibit at Momenta Lovett has participated in numerous exhibitions, including: Rush Art, NYC, Sculpture Center, NYC, and PS1 Contemporary Art Center, Long Island City, NY.

JUDE TALLICHET

Jude Tallichet's sound/sculpture installation, entitled *Two Wings to Go* unites architectural models and songs inspired by American gospel music. White architectural forms derived from suburban architecture of the midwestern United States double as speakers, projecting songs which have been composed and altered by Tallichet, combining her own configurations that produce it are bleakly humorous, boxy paradigms of stunted, self-satisfied pragmatism. It is the music that animates the space and provides the possibility of release and inspiration.

Jude Tallichet has an MA and an MFA from the University of Montana. She is a faculty member at Tyler School of Art,

compositions, arrangements, and lyrics. These speaker/models are electronically linked, seemingly singing to each other.

Each song embodies the social function of the building on which its sculpture is modeled. This architecture and the social

Philadelphia, PA. She has exhibited her work at P.S.1 Contemporary Art Center, Long Island City, NY. Following her exhibition at Momenta, Tallichet has exhibited with Artists Space, NYC, Jack Tilton Gallery, NYC, and Sara Meltzer's On View..., NYC.

MARY MAGSAMEN

Mary Magsamen's installation, entitled *Floater*, combines an instructional video on ballroom dancing with underwater photographs of scuba divers. Also included is a video of the artist dancing with a partner above water wearing scuba gear. This awkward physical comedy appears at first to be about the impossibility of communication and the inevitability of alienation. These satirical elements are disrupted by the reality of the scuba divers' clumsy, though somehow effective, interaction. Working as a team, each diver is dependent on the other for every breath, just as the dancers are dependent on each other for every step.

The instructional video is projected on the floor, creating a disorienting viewer participation. All approaches to the instructor are awkward due to the placement of the projector and by the fact that the viewer must cross the projector beam to examine the installation.

Mary Magsamen received an MFA from Cranbrook Academy of Art. She has exhibited her work at Anna Kustera Gallery, NYC, and White Columns, NYC. Since her exhibition at Momenta she has screened her videos and exhibited sculptures at various spaces, including PS122, NYC, Art in General, NYC, and The Knitting Factory, NYC.

YOUR UTOPIA

PETER FEND
GREGORY GREEN
KARA HAMMOND
JED BRAIN PICTURES
 PRESENTS ALBERT BUDD
DAVID SHAPIRO
DREW SHIFLETT
MIGUEL VENTURA

These artists explore grand visions of the future, reiterating and/or questioning avant-garde notions that art has the ability to transform society. *Your Utopia* implies a subjective definition of an ideal social construction. One person's utopia is another's hell on earth, human nature making shared utopia an impossibility. Artists in the exhibition display a wide range of approaches to this theme, often in conflict with each other. Some create futuristic artifacts based on historical references, some suggest sweeping political gestures, and others create fantastic architectural forms implying harmonious communities.

Peter Fend's wall piece, *Just Add Water (A Physical Examination of Joseph Beuys' Fat Corner)*, is a literal chemical breakdown of an historic artwork. Fend provides scientific evidence that Beuys' statement "everything must go through fat corner" is not a metaphor but a statement of fact. The "fat" in *Fat Corner* is actually paraffin, a stable combination of carbon, hydrogen and oxygen. Fend connects this compound to a *Triangle of Life* theory which states that these elements, combined with water, will produce life.

If art is reality, then Gregory Green's declaration of secession is not metaphor, but truth. Momenta Art officially seceded from the United States and joined the state of Caroline. All affiliates of Momenta received Caroline citizenship and the flag was displayed prominently outside the gallery door.

Miguel Ventura, *Exercises or Return of the Body, Language I*, 1998, two-channel video

David Shapiro, *The People's Sandal*, 1998, mixed media

Jed Brain Pictures Presents Albert Budd contributes a demo for the video game *Stabwoofie*. Developed on a game engine that has acquired an internet cult following, *Stabwoofie* is the manifestation of paranoid hallucinations based on the Kennedy assassinations made virtual.

While assassination proliferated, the space program became an important aspect of cultural identity. Kara Hammond's planet-scapes derived from outdated space probes celebrate the newly outdated. They remind us of the promise of a scientifically-devised utopia while exploring the history of the future.

Miguel Ventura's utopian vision is language-based. *Exercises or Return of the*

previous series, *The New Interterritorial Language Committee,* and appear to be an expression of the culture of an unspecified racial group. They are post-revolutionary instructions of the new etiquette.

The past implies the future in David Shapiro's *The People's Sandal:* a shoe display of tire sandals combined with Abbie Hoffman's *Steal This Book* and plastic model kits of the Vietcong. The ingenious efficiency of this fashion statement is combined with counterculture glamour derived from refuse.

A more positive contrast to these dark utopian visions is Drew Shiflett's *Walkway.* This architectural model/sculpture

JED BRAIN PICTURES PRESENTS ALBERT BUDD, *Stabwoofie*, 1998, video with mixed media

Body, Language I and Language IV are instructional videos based on glyph alphabets developed by the artist. These didactic primers are rooted in Ventura's

obsessively constructed of paper, wood and glue implies harmonious communities of the past, present, and future.

EL PUENTE:
MIND YOUR BUSINE$$

El Puente's installation titled *Mind Your Busine$$* is a collaborative installation examining youth culture, fashion and labor. El Puente Academy for Peace and Justice is a youth development center and public high school in Williamsburg, Brooklyn, that integrates art education into the students' curriculum through community-based,

working with Adjoa Jones De Almeida (English Facilitator), Joe Matunis, Josh Merrow and Patricia Montoya.

Under the direction of facilitators, the students worked on several projects, including: hand-painted playing cards; a documentary examining the garment

year-long projects. This year's project focuses on the garment industry and sweatshops. The installation presents an accumulation of projects in various media by students led by El Puente facilitators and resident artists, including Danny Hoch,

industry, which includes interviews with garment workers and investigative footage of conditions in sweatshops; performances of monologues written by the students relating to youth culture fashion; and personalized bikes made from recycled materials.

FACILITATOR-JOE MATUNIS, 1998,
Maquiladora Playingcards,
mixed media

Danny Hoch, El Puente Visiting Artist, is an Obie Award-winning writer and performer who recently presented his highly acclaimed solo show, *Jails, Hospitals & Hip-Hop.*

Joe Matunis, El Puente Arts Facilitator and founding member of the El Puente Academy for Peace and Justice, is a muralist who has directed large-scale mural projects in England, Scotland, India, and throughout the United States, and is currently completing a comic book called *Cupidity.*

Josh Merrow, El Puente Design Facilitator, is an inventor/sculptor and founder of *YAK Research*, an organization dedicated to making the world more pleasant.

Patricia Montoya, El Puente Video Facilitator, is a video-maker from Colombia and has screened her work at the Latin American Film and Video Festival in Toronto, Canada and the Gay and Lesbian Festival in New York City. She has also curated the Images Festival in Toronto, Canada.

FACILITATOR-JOSH MERROW, 1998,
Dream Machines, altered bicycles

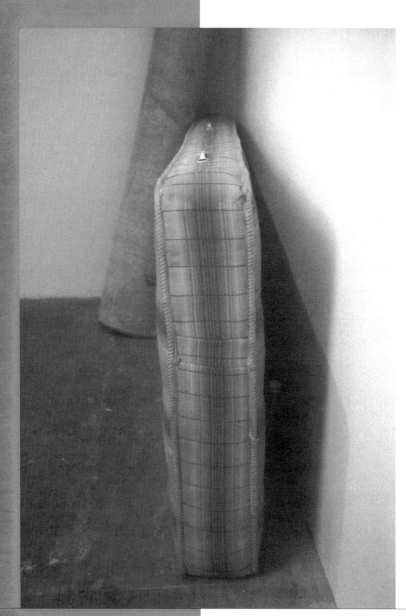

NICO JENKINS

Nico Jenkins's installation
Untitled(Searched Room) combines refuse
from a ransacked squat with photographs
taken in the same space. As we bear witness
to an unseen act, the elegant photographs
of the recently removed refuse operate as
both formal compositions and missing
evidence. These photos ask the viewer to
catalog the lives of the room's former
inhabitants as well as the destruction
caused by security forces and the artist.

A video of the destroyed building in Paris
provides further inconclusive evidence. Was
the building condemned by the authorities
or was it a terrorist target? What
relationship does the artist and/or the
viewer have to this unexplained, yet visually
appealing, destruction..

Nico Jenkins studied at Hunter College in
New York and received a BFA from San
Francisco Art Institute. He has exhibited
with Stephen Wirtz Gallery and Push Art
Space in San Francisco, CA, Galerie Fonz
Werner, Amsterdam, The Netherlands, and
has had solo exhibitions at Galerie
Titanuk, Turku, Finland and Chamber
Fine Arts, NYC.

MOMOYO TORIMITSU

Momoyo Torimitsu's installation *Danchizuma-Endless Sunrise,* operates as both portraiture and diorama. It is an artificial macro view of a Japanese "bed-town" (suburban sprawl) combined with candid photographs of its inhabitants. The artist examines the rise of uniform urbanism in Japan and its promise of harmony and production through the well-orchestrated lives of the *shufu (danchizuma).* Loosely translated, danchizuma means housewife, but in actuality there is no English equivalent for this particular societal role. She is a married woman whose place in society is both revered and ignored. We follow these brand-conscious yet nameless heroines through various scenarios in which life is a carefully choreographed journey through artificial gardens with palm trees, karaoke amusements, tennis circles and quasi-theme parks.

The diorama is an architectural model of an actual bed-town that exists in the shadow of Tokyo. Encased in a plastic bubble, each of its tiny lights represents a location where the photographs on the adjacent walls were taken. These lights invert the macro view from above and turn the gaze back to detail the inhabitation.

Momoyo Torimitsu is a graduate of Tama Art University and participated in the P.S.1 Contemporary Art Center International Studio Program in New York. Since her exhibition at Momenta, Torimitsu's work has been exhibited at : Jack Tilton Gallery, NYC, the Tate Gallery, London. and in a solo exhibition at Deitch Projects, NYC.

PAMELA LINS

"All the places we dream of going have always been accessible from the living room couch."

Pamela Lins's sculptures simultaneously allude to both traditional high art processes and recreational motifs. Odd combinations of carved urethane sports trophies and ice chests elevated on vented sculptural bases meld notions of leisure and connoisseurship. These objects allude to movement and travel, yet are strangely static and distant. They create a non-movement of vicarious spectatorship.

Lins is a graduate of Hunter College in New York. Her work has been exhibited at Thread Waxing Space, NYC, Brooklyn Museumof Art in Brooklyn, NY, and Ten in One Gallery, Chicago, IL. Following her exhibition at Momenta, Lins has exhibited with Blohard, Philadelphia, PA, Gallery Untitled, Dallas, TX, Andrew Kreps, NYC, Exit Art, NYC, White Columns, NYC, and Ten in One Gallery, NYC.

LIZA PHILLIPS

"...the sequence can involve much routine trial-and-error. Such maps of topography, however technical in execution, will continue to remain the constructs of human vision and judgment."
Dept. of the Interior, US Geological Survey, www.usgs.gov

Liza Phillips's paintings are derived from digital relief maps downloaded from the internet, remapped and enlarged onto panels using an airbrush. The paintings refuse to come into focus for the viewer, forcing an unresolvable abstract/topographical view of the earth and an uneasy alliance of depiction and abstraction.

Phillips is a graduate of Vassar College and the Chelsea College of Art and Design in London, and she has attended the Skowhegan Residency Program in Maine. Her work has been exhibited at Whitechapel Gallery, London, Weatherspoon Art Gallery, NC, and the Art Exchange Art Fair in NYC. Since her exhibition at Momenta, she has exhibited at the University Art Museum, California State University, San Bernardino, CA, Grand Central Art Center, Santa Ana, CA, Eyewash, Brooklyn, NY, and White Columns, NYC.

GEORGE COCHRANE

George Cochrane's paintings are derived from collaged images of historic figures combined with popular culture icons. The collaged photographs are transferred as graphite line drawings on a prepared oil ground. As Cochrane paints over the original line drawing, the identity of the sitter shifts and changes, creating a painterly narrative mirroring psychological tensions.

Cochrane's expressive paint handling is at contrast with the slick graphic imagery from which the paintings are derived. As the still familiar images of actors, fashion models and assassins are obscured, a leveling effect is created. The persons portrayed hold simultaneous identities.

George Cochrane has a BA from Sarah Lawrence College, and has exhibited with McKee Gallery in NYC and Guild Hall, East Hampton, NY.

PETER KRASHES

Peter Krashes's paintings present elegant handling of images derived from crude photographic distortions. Krashes's latest series of paintings is derived from photographs taken through distorted mirrors of constructed situations ranging from gatherings of friends to simple still lifes and physical therapy sessions. These violently distorted figures appear to be in the midst of a transformation - a transformation that seems both brutal and curative. Krashes's deft paint handling echoes the photographic distortions while increasing the tension through abstraction.

Peter Krashes received a BA from Middlebury College, attended the University of Oxford, New College, and received a BFA from the Ruskin School of Drawing and Fine Art. His work has been exhibited at Max Protetch, NYC, and Rare, NYC. Following his exhibition at Momenta, Krashes has exhibited at Aldrich Museum, Ridgefield, CT, Salon 300, Brooklyn, NY, and Guild Hall, East Hampton, NY.

HEIDI SCHLATTER

Heidi Schlatter's freestanding photographic props aretaken from a district in Panama City that was leveled by the US military during the invasion in 1989. These buildings are emptied of their history – they are the ordinary faces of any number of housing units around the world, ambiguous icons to progress, like anti-ads for a not-so-bright future.

Schlatter's vinyl enlargements of snapshots of these low-rent interiors and exteriors reveal a layer of uneasiness. The ordinary is twisted; like cutaways from graphic film scenes they describe places upon which the eye does not usually linger for very long. Using a medium commonly used for advertising, these innocuous places are blown out of proportion and mounted as free-standing elements. They exist as a thin skin between private space and public space, using the photographic image to distort one's perception of the exhibition space itself.

Heidi Schlatter received a BFA from Rhode Island School of Design, and attended Hunter College for her graduate studies. She has participated in numerous exhibitions, including *The Sculpture Center at Roosevelt Island*, NY, Long Island University Campus, Brooklyn, NY, *Nobodies Home* (see pages 64-65), Momenta Art, Brooklyn, NY, and P.S.1 Contemporary Art Center, Long Island City, NY.

LEE BOROSON

Lee Boroson's installation subverts the notion of architecture as a device to insulate culture from nature. Using fabric and false floors, Boroson transforms the gallery space into an intimate setting that redirects our gaze back to the space we occupy. The installation operates as a layer of insulation from the cold white cube surrounding it. A sheer curtain alludes to the transparency of

Lee Boroson received a BFA from State University of New York, New Paltz, NY, and an MFA from Indiana University, Bloomington, IN. His work has been included in exhibitions at Newhouse Center for Contemporary Art, Snug Harbor Cultural Arts Center, NY, and the Neuberger Museum, Purchase, NY. Following his exhibition at Momenta he

sky or water and takes the form of undulating, reactive walls that immediately contrast with the environment that supports them. The viewer's navigation through the gallery becomes consciously affected by the alterations to the space.

has exhibited at Whitney Museum at Champion, Stamford, CT, Joseph Helman, NYC, and has had solo exhibitions at Genovese/Sullivan Gallery, Boston, MA, and at the Whitney Museum of American Art at Phillip Morris, NYC.

NOBODIES HOME

Betty Beaumont, Michelle
Bertomen, David Boyle and
Brooklyn Architects Collective,
Hermann Gabler, Dan Graham,
Larry Krone, Allan McCollum,
Donna Nield, Mauricio Dias
and Walter Reidweg, Heidi
Schlatter, Peter Scott, Day
Gleason and Dennis Thomas,
Anton Vidokle

A group show concerned with living space
and alienation, curated by Peter Scott.
Catalog available, with contributions by
Betty Beaumont, Michelle Bertomen, Dan
Graham and Peter Scott.

Nobodies Home is a group exhibition
concerned with living space and alienation.
The exhibition takes its cue from the
current celebration of "lifestyle culture" so
prevalent in today's news and entertainment

Installation View (from left to right)
BETTY BEAUMONT, *Love Canal, USA,*
1978-1999, c-prints ANTON VIDOKLE,
Untitled (lounge chair), 1999, plastic
and metal PETER SCOTT, *Untitled
(bedroom)*, 1998, c-print and *Untitled
(bathroom)*,1999, c-print

media, where an endless parade of magazine
and television spots seems to reduce the
image of life to one of Martha Stewart's
hypnotic discourses on domesticity.

With television news offering tips on which supermarkets to avoid, and newspapers offering lengthy articles on how to find the right contractor for your Upper West Side renovation, the only significant problems these days seem to revolve around consumption and decoration. The artworks and texts for this exhibition have been chosen for their relevance to the alienation produced by an ever-expanding corporate capitalism that, in its tireless creation of new markets, is leaving an increasingly homogenized culture in its wake. Recognizing that this process is not taking place in a vacuum, the scope of the exhibition is intended to be broad enough to include reflections on shifts in economic and political agendas necessary to pave the way for the further progress of *The Society of the Spectacle* which, thirty years after Guy Debord first described the phenomenon, continues with what appears to be a renewed vengeance. For the most part reduced to playing the important but obsequious role of cheerleader to these events, the major media, dependent on advertising revenue which in turn requires the allegiance of consumers, has become extremely adept at stimulating the public's fears and desires in a largely successful bid to distract it from any doubts that might develop during infrequent moments of quiet reflection. *Nobodies Home* might be seen, in part, as an effort to entertain these doubts and expand upon them.

The artists chosen for this exhibition are not necessarily chosen because their work subscribes to its premise but on the basis of specific pieces that might, when seen in the overall context of the show, loosely describe the alienating effects these conditions might have on our cultural experience of a home. *Peter Scott*

DAN GRAHAM, *Alteration to a Suburban House,* 1976-1999, digital c-print

BANKS VIOLETTE

Banks Violette's untitled installation, comprised of an oil-on-linen painting and two chandeliers doubling as incendiary devices, is a fairyland armageddon sutured from the landscape of a (provisional) American history. Using such diverse references as Motorhead album covers, Breughel, and pathological teenage gangs, Violette weaves popular culture

members of the Magic Kingdom in order to infiltrate Disney World and randomly execute tourists, but were arrested before their plans could be realized. Violette's chandeliers mirror this pathological non-event. As the juveniles take on one fiction to assault another, so does the painting *Untitled (L.O.C.)*. This intricate and layered landscape presents conventions of adolescent fantasy and bloodlust to the point of collapse.

iconography into an operatic tale of co-opted rebellion. The chandeliers, from the series *Descendent Aggressor*, are named after members of the extremist juvenile delinquent club *The Lords of Chaos*. They planned to disguise themselves as

Banks Violette received a BA from the School of Visual Arts, NYC and attended Columbia University's MFA Program. After his exhibition at Momenta, his work was exhibited at Team Gallery, NYC.

RACHEL LOWTHER

Rachel Lowther's untitled installation of related sculptures and drawings weave a nonlinear narrative of frozen gestures. The three drawings are encased in hand-carved wooden frames inspired by Van Eyck's *Last Judgment*. Dense, apocalyptic and silent, each drawing centers around a male figure. In order to fully enter the installation the viewer must step over a site-specific three-dimensional line of black plaster, as well as a roughly articulated severed head made of wax and encrusted with feathers. These repressed yet animalistic gestures are bracketed by two resin ospreys perched high on the gallery walls. As overseers to this open-ended narrative, their gaze appears icy, unyielding, cruel, and almost human.

Rachel Lowther received her MFA from Hunter College, NYC, and also attended Stadelschule, Frankfurt, Germany, and Chelsea College of Art and Design, London. She has exhibited her work at Sculpture Center, NYC, Bronwyn Keenan, NYC, Yearsley Spring Gallery, Philadelphia, PA, and The Approach, London.

ACKNOWLEDGEMENTS

This catalog is dedicated to the memories of Robert Blanchon and David Gilmore.

Momenta Art is a not-for-profit exhibition space whose mission is to promote the work of emerging artists through two person shows, providing artists separate project rooms and the distinct opportunity to present a substantial body of work. This catalog was made possible through the generous support of The Florence J. Gould Foundation, Ms. Agnes Gund and Mr. Daniel Shapiro, and The Heathcote Foundation.

Sponsors: Brooklyn Borough President Howard Golden, Gabriella De Ferrari, Experimental Television Workshop LTD, Ronald and Frayda Feldman, The Greenwall Foundation, The Florence J. Gould Foundation, Ms. Agnes Gund and Mr. Daniel Shapiro, The Heathcote Foundation, Janet Heist, The Jerome Foundation, Materials for the Arts, NYC Department of Cultural Affairs, New York State Council on the Arts, White Columns, Anne M. Young
Contributors: Jennifer Cohen, Kara Hammond, Evan Kingsley and Dara Meyers-Kingsley, Marvin Pasternak, Noreen Shipman, Cindy Sherman
Founding Members: Donna Czapiga, James Mills
Board of Directors: Michael Ashkin, Laura Cottingham, Jody Culkin, James Elaine, Kathleen Goncharov, Eric Heist, Peter Hopkins, Laura Parnes, Calvin Reid, Anne M. Young
Advisory Committee: Christine Davis, Amy Ben-Ezra, Barry Hylton, O. Donald Odita
Directors: Eric Heist, Laura Parnes
Assistant Director: Jenny Frances Martin

Momenta Art
72 Berry Street
Brooklyn, NY 11211
tel/fax 718.218.8058

This is a publication of Momenta Art.

Designed by Sarah Vogwill
Edited by Michael Ashkin

Manufactured in the United States.